Psychic Beauty

~ Energy Cords & Psychic Exercises ~

By Kelliena

iUniverse, Inc.
Bloomington

iUniverse books may be ordered through booksellers or by contacting:

iUniverse
1663 Liberty Drive
Bloomington, IN 47403
www.iuniverse.com
1-800-Authors (1-800-288-4677)

ISBN: 978-1-4620-3384-3 (sc)
ISBN: 978-1-4620-3385-0 (e)

www.kelliena.com

Printed in the United States of America

iUniverse rev. date: 07/22/2011

An eternity of gratitude to the Divine, Angels, Guardians and Fairies.

Thank-you to my beautiful sisters, Tracy and Kim, my best friends and soul sisters!

Thank-you to Mum and Dad for your understanding and faith in me.

Thank-you to Nannie Jessie for believing in me. Rest in peace.

Thank-you to my 'Brother' Josh and Sister-in-law Gina and baby Isabella.

Thank-you to The Ryan Sisters for your constant support and inspiring music.

Thank-you to Yvette d'Entremont for guiding me through the editing process. Thank-you for your patience.

Thank-you to Little Mysteries Vanessa, Sandra, Amanda, Renee, Amy, Kristin and Jenna.

Thank-you to Sarah's Spiritual Treasures, Sarah, Tom, John and Kyle.

Thank-you to Melissa for your help.

Thank-you to Fairy Princess Phyllie, for being you.

Thank-you to Phyllis Laforest and Darlene "Mighty One" for being my Idols.

Thank-you to our Fiery 'Aunt Colette'.

Thank-you to Ann Costello, Deirdre and Aisling Porter. I am so honored to have met you.

Thank-you to Jasmin for your energy.

Thank-you to Caitlyn Colford my gifted photographer.

Thank-you to all my friends, family and Seekers for your continued support.

For all Seekers

Intro

My intention with this book is to prove to you that **you** have an inner Divine power to read energy and speak with the Universe.

You have always had the power. It is in your heart.

Energy Cords are not set in stone. The examples and descriptions given in this book are based on my personal experience working with the Energy Cords. Energy Cords may be presented differently to you, but the principle behind it is the same.

It is important for you to make these techniques your own. If you do not connect with a psychic exercise or feel that you need to do it differently, please trust this. Also, if you feel the need to add or combine elements to an exercise, please do.

The Energy Cords

What is an Energy Cord?

An Energy Cord is the Energy path that comes from the Soul or Divine and it connects us to everything.

There are four classifications of Cords: Energy Cords, Soul Cords, Guardian Cords and Ego Cords.

The Cords are a type of energy connecting everyone. We are all surrounded by them. This book will focus on two cords - **Energy Cords** and **Ego Cords**. These Cords are attached to everyone and they are part of you.

For example, just like how your blood carries important nutrients to the cells in your body, the Energy Cords are carrying important messages to your Soul. Energy Cords are from the Divine and have very particular meanings. They are part of who we **ARE**.

The Ego Cords on the other hand are the manifestation of what we are **NOT**. Ego Cords are similar to the cholesterol that can build up and block your arteries. Ego Cords can block the natural flow of the Energy Cords. The two classifications are further broken down into more specific energies - i.e. Fire Cords, Mountain Cords, etc.

An explanation of these two classifications are as follows:

Energy Cords appear as rays of light encircling the Seeker. These Cords are like a weather "energy" forecast. They are quite changeable. The Seeker is drawn to this particular weather element.

For example, if Fire Cords are shown, the Seeker has perhaps been burning more candles or incense recently.

Ego Cords are the Cords that teach us what we are not.

The other two Cords that I will mention are:

Soul Cords (Basic) are the Cords that represent what the Seekers truly are. It is the Soul's Truth. The Cord comes from the Seeker in a lateral pattern. I see it shooting out from the chest area. It tends to show up behind the Seeker as well, suggesting that this Soul has fulfilled this role many times. For example, if the Guardians are presenting a Healers Cord, you may see the energy cord shoot straight behind the Seeker. This lets the Reader know that he/she had an "active" healer role in a past life.

To 'activate' a Soul's Cord, the Seeker must walk their true path and be true to their own heart.

Guardian Cords are the Cords of the Guardians. They are much more mobile and diverse than the other Cords. Soul Cords appear more connected to the Seeker, while Energy Cords are more of a broad beam of light in varying shapes and sizes.

The Reading

How do I work and how have I come to understand Energy Cords? Ever since I can remember, I have seen these lights or cords. It is part of my every waking moment.

I have been told that seeing these cords is "different" and not the "normal" experience. I, however, disagree. I know everyone has the ability to see these Cords in their own way. It is very easy to dismiss these lights and think instead that it may have been a passing car or even just in your imagination.

The Early Years

Even as a young child, I saw Energy and many Guardians. I did not know I was different nor did I consider myself a psychic. I do not believe that being psychic is special. Everyone is psychic.

I hope that this book will help you believe in your own psychic powers.

Throughout elementary school I was belittled by my peers. I was constantly teased and bullied by many members of the popular crowd. My experiences taught me that if I did not react, the kids would forget about me. This early childhood experience taught me not to have any expectations of others nor to care about what others think about me. The summer before my first year in junior high school, I remember the Guardians coming to me and helping me set my energy so that I could make friends and be more accepted.

I also did this by focusing my intension. I wanted to have the confidence to speak to the other children, and then planned a new look for myself (I had a very nifty perm). I practiced speaking and wrote a list of things to talk about when meeting new friends.

My first day at junior high school, I was 13 years old and very excited to attend my first 'Sock Off' (dance). I remember feeling really grown up and elated that I was becoming a teen. With the white light surrounding me and my Guardians by my side, I walked up to a girl, Isabella (not her real name). She was also standing on her own in the gym. I introduced myself. This was a first for me; I was accepted by one of my peers. The Light had given me a gentle confidence to speak.

After a fun morning of new classes and introductions, the afternoon Sock Off was approaching. I remember running home to put on make up. When I got back, the dark gym and dancing lights made it much easier to see the energies and Guardians.

Isabella and I were standing next to each other when I noticed two HUGE Guardians opening a door of green light to release energy. (I am not sure what type of energy). I turned to Isabella, pointed to the energy and asked her why were they doing that?

She looked at me as if I was losing it and asked me "What are you talking about??"
Under what I call the 'Energy Door" were a group of well known bullies. They had noticed me pointing to them. Six or seven girls marched up to Isabella and I and asked "What the F$%^ are you pointing at?"

This was the moment that I realized "wait, they don't see this". It was this precise moment that I realized I was the only one who was seeing these Angelic Beings. Very red faced I awkwardly said in a shaky voice "I am so sorry, I thought I saw a friend."

It was my understanding that the two huge Guardians were watching. They helped remove any 'EGO' energy from the girls so they were okay with my answer. They went back to their corner.

That night I was in a bit of shock and went to bed early.

I asked the Divine 'Why didn't they see them?' and 'Why didn't I know?'

I was not angry with anyone, just very confused.

A single ray of white light in gold trim presented herself to me and said:

"You have a responsibility."

She then said (I can't remember word for word but basically it went like this):

"You needed to learn that you must go by your own heart, not by the 'popular' crowds at school."

Then she asked me what I wanted to do with this life?

I asked her if I could help everyone.

Then the White light disappeared, but I felt a very strong sense of deep love and I could smell roses.

This was the beginning of my "lessons" from the Guardians.

Everyone has this ability. Throughout this book, I will share my experiences and understanding of these energies. I will also share the psychic exercises that have been shown to me or that I have created based on my own energy. I am going to show you how I start 'focusing' my sight to see clearer. Again, please remember to make all of these suggestions your own.

How Guardian Cords appear to me depends on who is present. They step in as a wisp of smoke and then transform into the light declaring who they are. They appear as Angels, Fairies, Merfolk and other Divine Beings. This may be different for each individual. For simplicity's sake, throughout this book I will refer to them as 'Guardians.'

Before a Reading I always "raise" a golden circle (see page 76) with the intention that while using my intuition, whatever messages are presented to me must be for the Highest Good of the Seeker and Divine. Every reading I do is to empower the Seekers and help remind them of their own gifts.

Before the Seeker physically crosses the **golden circle,** the Energy Cords will cross the golden Cord first. This gives me an idea of where the Seeker's energy is. When a Seeker physically crosses the Golden Circle, his/her Soul Cords begin to resemble illuminated spider webs of light.

I then read the Seeker's energy. Once the Cords are read, the information is given to the Seeker. The Guardian Cords will then appear as entities and gently pull one of the Seeker's Soul Cords with a message they want me to focus on.

For example, if they want the Seeker to realize that they are a Healer, the Guardian Cord will hold the Healer's Cord and the Guardian Cord will then magnify this Cord in front of me as though the string is being placed under a microscope. Inside the Cord are symbols and messages meant for the Seeker. Often these symbols do not make sense immediately. However with time the Seeker will come to understand their Guardian's messages.

The symbols are a coding system the Guardians use to communicate with the Seeker. For example, one Seeker came to me and was asking about a man she was seeing. A Fairy came forward and presented an image in my third eye of a picture of the Seeker, a huge penny, and the gentleman she was seeing. The Fairy's message was that there was money between them. When I told the Seeker what the Fairy said, she stated that they never exchanged money. So I looked at the Fairy and the Fairy told me to ask the Seeker about her work. The Seeker said that she met her boyfriend at the bank. The Seeker's Fairy used a penny to represent the bank. The bank represented the place where the Seeker met this gentleman; it is how they are connected.

Once the Guardian Cord(s) have shown the Cord they wish the Seeker will focus on, the reading becomes focused on the energy in front of the Seeker.

For example, if a Seeker is working in a Moon energy, the Guardian may say "The fire is raising before the Seeker," which means that things are going to be very fast paced, but cleansing.

Another type of Cord that the Guardian Cord may focus on are Travel Cords. These Cords are usually represented by a brown Cord that looks like a rope. This Cord is usually connected to the Seeker's hand (either right or left).

I've asked the Guardian Cord if there is any significance between the right or left hand, but they have said that it is just the direction the Seeker is headed. Left is a very intuitive path, while the right is what you are forging on your own. On the other side of this Cord is a map. The map normally looks like a hand drawn, antique map. Sometimes Guardians will mention cities. The more you read energies, the more you recognize the energy of cities. It is very hard to explain city Cords. You may see a flash of a well known building or a road sign.

To conclude the readings, the Guardians will repeat what they feel is the most important message the Seeker needs to remember. Please keep in mind that this may not answer what the Seeker originally asked. Guardians have a habit of addressing only what they feel is most important to the Seeker at that moment. For example, if you came for a reading to ask about romance, but the Guardians feel that you do not see yourself properly, they may not answer your question directly. They may instead focus on your own gifts to empower you.

You may therefore feel that you are not getting a response from them. This is usually because they believe you have not completed your "homework" (i.e. a task they have given you).

They are like pieces of a puzzle that you need to complete yourself. If the Guardians give you advice on how to put two pieces together, and you do not follow through, they will wait until you complete the task before giving you your next "assignment."

Let's say in your heart you feel as though you need to contact an old friend but have not done so. The Guardians will keep at you, reminding you to contact your old friend, before providing you with another message.

Understanding the Elements

These are my two understandings of Elements:

1. The Guardians of the Elements. They are great Teachers and Masters of the element energy. For example, let's imagine you are meditating by candlelight. If while gazing at the candle you see a string of fire burst from the flame, chances are that's the Guardian of that element.

2. The energy itself of each element. More simply put, if you're using a candle flame to meditate, you're using the fire element to focus your psychic sight.

When working with the elements remember that they are Souls too. They are NOT yours to command.

Air:

Physical Representation:

Feathers
Incense
Smoke

Key words:

Words
Mental

Communication

When to work with Air:

Air helps us connect with our mental energy. Air is an excellent Energy to work with if you need to clear your mind or clear out old Energy that you have outgrown.

Also Air is excellent Energy to use when you need to write or communicate.

This exercise will help you "program" the smoke as a telephone between you and your Guardians.

What you will need:

A lighter/match
Stick of Incense (whatever scent you feel connected to at the moment)
An Incense holder
Pen
Paper
A candle and candle holder (optional)

The psychic exercise:

1.   In a semi dark room find a comfortable place to sit

2.   Place the stick of incense in the holder

3.   As you light the incense, invite your Guardians or Loved Ones who have crossed over to your circle.

4.   Focus a Cord of energy from the Chakra that you wish to use. (please see page 75)

5.   Begin to program the smoke.

6.   For each direction before you declare a message theme.

Write out each smoke symbol meaning on a piece of paper as the following:

Counterclockwise circles mean	_____
Clockwise circles mean	_____
Straight smoke mean	_____
Wavy smoke mean	_____
Going left mean	_____
Going right mean	_____

*** For the definition of each go with your heart. This is your 'telephone.' Make it your own. ***

The Exercise (AIR):

Take a few deep breaths and again focus on your Cords and ask the Guardians your questions.

Please be sure to give thanks after every answer given.

If you feel that you are not receiving any answers, it maybe because they feel you have all the information you need at this time.

~~~~~~

Fire

Physical Representation:

Candles
Fire places
Camp fires

Key words:

Breakthrough
Spiritual
Focus

When to work with Fire:
Fire is an excellent Energy to call upon when you need a positive change and/or breakthrough.

Also Fire can help us find inspiration and help reconnect us to our higher spiritual self.

What you will need:

Candle
Lighter
Candle holder

The psychic exercise:

1. In a dark room place the candle in the holder and connect your third eye with the Cord you wish to work with to the flame

2. For each direction of the flame declare a message theme.

Write out each flame symbol on a piece of paper as the following:

Flame with quick 'flickers' mean	_____
Flame with slow 'flickers' mean	_____
Flame burning to the left mean	_____
Flame burning to the right mean	_____
Flame standing still mean	_____

*** For the definition of each go with your heart. This is your 'telephone.' Make it your own. ***

The Exercise (FIRE):

Take a few deep breaths and again focus on your Cords and ask your Guardians your questions.

Please be sure to give thanks after every answer that's given.

If you feel that you are not receiving any answers, it may be because they feel you have all the information you need at this time.

~~~~~~

Water:

Physical Representation:

Ocean
River
Lake
Rain

Key words:

Dreams
Emotional
Psychic

When to work with Water:

Water is a beautiful Energy to work with when you are ready to connect with the Dream World and/or Past lives.

Also Water can help us reconnect with our Soul mates.

What you will need:

A Clear Glass bowl
Water (to Fill the Bowl)

A Tea light
Candle holder
Dark Room
Table

Preparing for the exercise:

1. Fill your bowl roughly half way with water.

2. In a dark room find a comfortable place to sit

3. Place the candle in the holder

4. As you light the candle invite your Guardians or Loved Ones who have crossed over to your circle.

5. Focus the Cord you wish to work with from the Chakra that you which to use.

6. Place the lit candle on the table

7. Place the bowl of water between you and the candle.

8. Sit before the flame and water so that you are able to see through the bowl of water to the candle flame.

The Exercise (WATER):

Focus on softening your gaze on the Flame as you look through the bowl of water.

Humbly ask for messages for the highest good.

Keep an open mind to the images before you and makes notes of the symbols or visions that are presented to you.

Give thanks.

** If you see nothing then you already have all the information you need at that time.
~~~~~~

Earth:

Physical Representation:

Crystals
Earth

Key words:

Physical
Grounded
Building

When to work with Earth:

Earth is a brilliant Energy the helps us build our path.

Is also helps keep us grounded when we lose our focus.

What you will need:

Any crystal of your choice.

Preparing for the exercise:

Take the Crystal in your hand and focus the Cord of your choice from the Chakra that you wish to work with.

The Exercise (EARTH):

Visualize your Cords wrapping around this crystal and visualize your Cords integrating your Energy with the Crystal's Energy. Ask the Guardians to work with you to help you with your path or question.

Take a few deep breathes and feel the energy work with you. Please be sure to make note of any message or feelings.

Key notes when working with the Element Guardians or Energies

- Build a loving friendship with them.

- Listen to everything.

- Have NO expectations

- Give thanks

~~~~~~

Avoids Table

Air	Fire	Water	Earth
Laziness	Crowds	Gossip	Being in a rush
Staying up to late	Talking too much	Complaining	Too much Caffeine
Negative words	Thinking too much	Worrying	Being indoors too much

Soul's Light and Ego

When I was about 6 years old, a very kind Guardian came to me in a dream. He showed me a white marble circular room supported by many high pillars. This room was in the middle of forest with the biggest trees I had ever seen.

The forest seemed to be singing.

The Guardian took me to a huge basin made of moonlight. In this basin he showed me two rays of light.

The First Cord was a ray of changing colours and textures.

He explained this was **true** Soul's Light. It is what all Souls truly are. No Soul is defined by its body.

The second Cord was a smoky brown that reminded me of a river after a heavy rain storm.

The Guardian said this was **false** Soul's light. I later dubbed it Ego. This light tries to convince True Soul's light of its lies.

Every Soul on Earth is to master and understand its false Soul's light so as not to be blinded by it.

~~~~~~

When doing any readings or energy work it is very important to understand the difference between Soul's Light and Ego.

Soul's Light is our Divine higher self. It is who you truly are. Whenever you feel you are 'missing' something from your life's path, refocus your Soul's Light.

Ego teaches us what we are not. Ego places fear, anger and Judgement in a Seeker's heart.

Soul's-light	Ego
Love	Fear
Empowerment	Worry
Joy	Anger
Clear understanding	Frustration
Healing	Judgement of others or yourself

Every reading should provide the Seeker with an understanding of their power and give them the tools to help manage the energy around them.

If you are doing a reading on yourself, you may often feel that that you are 'seeing' what you wish to see.

To help give you the confidence in your OWN reading, you can program your Energy Cords before the session.

To program your Reading:

1. Visualize your Soul's Light.

2. Take a few very deep breaths and humbly invite your Guardian into your Soul's light.

3. Ask that every Cord be connected to the Divine's truth. Request that every word, energy, feeling, etc. presented to you is nothing but the truth for the highest good. You want to ensure that instead of being caught up in ego, you are seeing the true root of that Cord.

4. Give thanks and have faith in the Divine and your power.

Quiz: What Energy Cord you are working on?

**Please remember that these can change quite quickly and that you may be working with more than one Energy Cord.

Question 1

Do you feel (either night now or about life in general) that you:

(A)   Can't sit still
(B)   Are stuck
(C)   Are experiencing emotions that are up and down
(D)   Are NOT being heard
(E)   Need your own space

If you answer:

(A)   Please go to Question 2
(B)   Please go to Question 3
(C)   Please go to Question 4
(D)   Please go to Question 5
(E)   Please go to Question 6

Question 2

Right now when you are interacting with others your energy is:

(A)   Joyful
(B)   Intense
(C)   Scattered

If You Answer:

(A)   You are in a Sun Cord
(B)   You are in a Fire Cord
(C)   You are in a Volcano Cord

Question 3

Do you find the energy before you go to sleep:

(A)   Accomplished
(B)   Searching for something....
(C)   Need to be outdoors
(D)   Wanting to have fun

If You Answer:

(A) You are in a Mountain Cord
(B) You are in a Tree Cord
(C) You are in a Earth Cord
(D) You are in a Snow Cord

Question 4

In the morning the first thing you need to do is:

(A) Drink water/tea/coffee
(B) Shower
(C) Hit the snooze button
(D) Hope this day is a happy change from yesterday...

If You Answer:

(A) You are in a Ocean Cord
(B) You are in a River Cord
(C) You are in a Lake Cord
(D) You are in a Rain Cord

Question 5

Lately you have been 'gathering' information by:

(A) Meditating more
(B) Looking at a stressful situation from everyone else's point of view
(C) Patiently waiting for the Divine to give it to you
(D) Internet
(E) Asking your close friends
(F) Listening to everyone and everything

If You Answer:

(A) You are in a Starlight Cord
(B) You are in a Sky Cord
(C) You are in a Flower Cord
(D) You are in a Feather Cord
(E) You are in a Smoke Cord
(F) You are in a Wind Cord

Question 6

Your spiritual practice has been:

(A) Your own personal meditations
(B) You have been having visions
(C) 'Jumping' from one teacher to an other
(D) Feel the need to seek out a new teacher
(E) What is a 'spiritual practice?'

If You Answer:

(A) You are in a Moonlight Cord
(B) You are in a Star Cord
(C) You are in a Rainbow Cord
(D) You are in a Crystal Cord
(E) You are in an Ice Cord

Energy Cords table

Fire	Earth	Air	Water	Spirit
Sun Joyful Discovery Secrets Reward	**Mountains** Overcoming obstacles. Needs to seek out more information.	**Starlight** Higher wisdom. Dreams Divine connections.	**Ocean** Strong connection to the Ocean, Merfolk, and Dreams	**Moonlight** Moon connections. Goddess High Priestess
Fire Spiritual Focus Business Clearing of energy.	**Tree** Nature Eat more beans. Family	**Sky** Seeing the whole picture. Birds Calm	**River** Feels the need for change. Movement Change of home	**Star** High Spiritual gifts. Works with the Elements. Peace
Volcano Breakthrough Profound change.	**Earth** Grounding Crystals Dancing	**Flowers** Guardians Patience Be Gentle	**Lake** Be Still Information at a standstill. Swimming	**Rainbow** Peace maker Many cultures Past life work
	Snow Focus on your connection to the Divine. Winter sports	**Feather** Writing Arts Communication	**Rain** Washing away old energy. You are healing. Spring is here	**Crystal** Teacher Councillor to others. Abundance
		Smoke Psychic upgrade. Energy Shift Lower energy		**Ice** Energy 'frozen' Disappointment may be a blessing in disguise.
		Wind Listen Music Creative		**Spirits** The Soul's Cords of others

Energy Cords

East/Air

On Wednesday April 1, 2009 the Guardians woke me up and asked me to get an accounting program. I said I would.

I went to the store and the first program I saw was $399.99. I thought It was a bit expensive but I figured the Guardians know what they are talking about. The Next one I saw was for $499.99. I said to the Guardians "Ummm are you sure this is where you want me to get it?" They said 'yes'.

I kept looking and the next one I saw was $99.99. I thought it was better, but the Guardians said to keep looking. I found one for $29.99. I was super excited!

When I took it to cash it rang up $79.99. I told the gentleman (who was very nice) that I thought it was $29.99, but I could be wrong. So we checked it and there were five signs for $29.99 and one sign for $79.99. The Cashier gave it to me for $29.99! The Guardians knew I needed help managing my finances.

Air helps us communicate with our Spirit

Mercury

The Element of Air helps us understand our mental energy. Everyone has a "**Mercury Cord**" (p. 69) which helps us understand the "East/Air Cords" that surrounds us.

Often we receive important "East/Air Cords" through newspapers, magazines or other printed words.

East/Air

The Element of Air is quick and helps us focus on communications of mind, body and Spirit.

Common Blocks:

- Don't feel your truth is being heard.
- Assuming the truth
- Speaking or acting using one's ego.

Star Light Cords:

These Cords are like thin rays of starlight and are a bit thicker than most Cords.

Seeing these Cords signifies this is a time of higher knowledge for the Seeker. The Seeker is receiving messages from the Divine that may not make "conscious" sense. It's very important for the Seeker to pay attention to every sign during the reading.

The Seeker may notice they want to sleep in the mornings and stay up late at night.

Key Characteristics of Star Light Cords:

Food to eat: Home cooked meals

Energies to avoid: Fast food restaurants

Psychic Exercise: On a clear night, either go outside and find a comfy spot or position yourself near a picture window in a comfy chair. Focus on your Third Eye[1] until you feel the energy tingling. Visualize an Energy Cord of starlight coming from your Third Eye that shoots out to the stars. Listen intently for any messages or any energy that's returned.

---

1   The Third Eye is the Chakra located just above and between your physical eyes. It is the energy point that helps you see between worlds.

Sky Cords:

There is no actual Cord. Instead you will see an open blue sky. This represents you, the Seeker, conscientiously trying to view a stressful/intense situation from a higher perspective. The Seeker is being held accountable for his/her words or actions. This is excellent energy to pursue a writing project (i.e. journaling, writing stories, etc.).

Key Characteristics of Sky Cords:

Food to eat: Blueberries

Energies to avoid: Being underground (i.e. basements)

Psychic Exercise: Visualize a white Cord coming from your third eye. Find a cloud to which you feel connected and focus your Energy Cord on connecting with the cloud. Be sure to ask if it is okay with the cloud (it is a Spirit too). Stare at the cloud and listen carefully.

Flower Cords

Key Characteristics of Flower Cords:

These Cords are usually presented as flowers or a bouquet in one's Aura. If the flowers are displayed outside of the aura, the Seeker should buy himself/herself some flowers. Flower Cords are presented when the Divine wishes the Seeker to recognize his/her inner and outer beauty (within and without). This is an excellent time for the Seeker to treat themselves to a massage or Reiki/Energy treatment.

Food to eat: Any green vegetable

Energies to avoid: Being indoors too long (ex. prolonged computer usage)

Psychic exercise: Work in a garden where you will place crystals. To do this, use your energy to pick a crystal that feels right for your flowers and trees.

Be sure to invite the Guardians to your garden and give thanks.

Note In the winter, buy yourself a bouquet of flowers. Put crystals in the vase or surrounding the vase.

Feather Cords

Key Characteristics of Feather Cords:

These Cords normally appear as a puff of smoke, but in the shape of a feather. If the Seeker knows the type of bird the feather comes from, then the Guardians will ask the Seeker to pay attention to this type of bird for guidance. For example, a black feather is usually a crow. Crows represent magic and higher wisdom. The Seeker may have noticed the presence of many crows in recent times. If you the Seeker sees them, you should interpret these birds as "giving them a thumbs up." You are on the right path!

If I as the Reader cannot pinpoint to which bird the feather belongs, I ask the Seeker to meditate on the matter for further insight.

If the Reader sees the feather appear as fuzzy or blurry, it's a strong warning the Seeker avoid gossip and complaining.

This is an excellent time for the Seeker to write.

Food to eat: Rice (white or brown)

Energies to avoid: Crowded malls and gossip

Psychic Exercise: Take a walk around your yard or local park and see if you find any feathers. Remember that finding a feather is a gift from the birds. Give tobacco or anything else to show your respect for the birds and Air Guardians.

Smoke Cords

Key Characteristics of Smoke Cords:

As the name suggests, these Cords are usually presented as a column of smoke. This smoke represents a psychic upgrade for the Seeker. Sometimes the Seeker may feel that his/her physical energy is low during this upgrade period.

Food to eat: Smoked meat, smoked fish, smoked tofu.

Energies to avoid: Negative words

Psychic Exercise: As you burn incense, focus a loving white light from your third eye to the smoke. Give thanks to the Air Guardians and ask it they have any messages for you.

Wind Cords

Key Characteristics of Wind Cords:

These Cords are not visual. Instead they are more of a haze of silver that appears briefly and are not really full cord. The Reader may hear a gust of wind in his/her ear. The Seeker is normally guided to be still and listen because this indicates that there are positive changes coming his/her way.

Food to eat: Bean sprouts

Energies to avoid: Loud noises.

Psychic Exercise: Sit outside and listen to the wind and birds. Focus your energy on everything the wind touches; the trees, the clothes on the line, etc. Listen for your message and give thanks.

Energy Cords

South/Fire

On January 31st, 2001, I entered a beautiful New Age Store called Little Mysteries in Halifax, Nova Scotia. I remember the sense of entering a very sacred space. I'd never been in this store before, and I didn't know where to look. When I gazed at the very back of the store on the right hand side, I saw a silver sparkle in the corner before the sparkles returned to the far wall. I went to see what the Guardian wanted me to look at.
It was a book about Candlemas.

On February 2nd is a celebration called Imbolc, which means the return of the Light. The Guardian wanted me to refocus my spiritual path using this book as a guide. This was a significant moment for me since I realized I needed to focus and become very serious about my Life's path.

Fire helps us understand our Spiritual Energy.

South/Fire

The Element of Fire is a strong and passionate energy. It helps us with spiritual practice and business.

When balanced, fire can help break through illusions and deceit. However, when a Seekers fire becomes unbalanced it can blind your Soul's-light.

Common Blocks:

- Not enough focus
- Can't sit still

Sunlight Cords:

These Cords are presented as a thin ray of sunlight. This indicates a very joyful time for the Seeker. The Seeker is asked to recognize his/her hard work. The Guardians or Guardians may present a number with this Cord. For example, if a Fairy shows a 3 that is written in Sunlight that could mean that the past 3 days, 3 weeks or 3 months have been a period of reward.

These Seekers should remain in the moment and focus only on what makes them laugh and what inspires joy.

Key Characteristics of Sunlight Cords:

Food to eat:

- Starfruit
- Pineapple
- Oranges

Energies to avoid:

- Web surfing for more than an hour

Psychic Exercise: Lay in the sun (either indoors or outdoors). Close your eyes and allow the heat of the sun to go through you. Taking deep breaths, visualize the sunlight. This helps remove ego energy from your body, mind and spirit.

Fire Cords

Key Characteristics of Fire Cords:

These Cords are very bright and strong ropes of fire. The reader may feel a wave of heat coming from the Seeker. This represents an energy of spiritual knowledge. It also means the Seeker has a gift for business. It is important that the Seeker keep all words and actions very positive.

The Seeker has strong sight and will be able to read the energy surrounding them.

It may be wise for the Seeker to do Candle meditations.

Food to eat: Spicy food and chocolate

Energies to avoid: N/A

Psychic Exercise: Sitting in a quiet, dark room invite the Guardians of Fire, your Guardians to help you clear your energy.

Light a candle

From the Chakra of your choice, visualize an Energy Cord of fire connecting your energy to the candle's flame.

Speak to the fire silently or aloud about what you need to cleanse. Visualize the flame surrounding your body, eliminating any energy blocks or Ego energy.

Give Thanks. ** It may be wise to light an incense stick as an offering during or after this exercise. Do whatever you as the Seeker feels is appropriate **

Volcano Cords

Key Characteristics of Volcano Cords:

These Cords present themselves in the image of a volcano in your mind's eye.
It is very important to focus on the image as the energy is presenting itself.

Dormant
Gentle flow of Lava
Exploding volcano

This Cord of energy presents itself when a Seeker is breaking through 'major' energy blocks.

Food to eat: Anything spicy

Energies to avoid: Complaints

Psychic Exercise: To break an 'energy block'

Give an image to your block. If you are frustrated that you are not being heard, visualize an ear with a shell or armor on it.

From the Chakra that you wish to use, visualize and focus on a Fire Cord coming from the centre of your Chakra.

Focus on a volcano. You can even get a picture of one if you like. Ask the energy from the volcano to help you break this energy block.

Energy Cords

West/Water

My Sister Tracy has the gift of dreams. One of her first visions was when she was 12 years old and she dreamed about our Great Grandmother. In my sister's dream, she was downstairs playing while our Mother was in the laundry room folding clothes. The ceiling lit up and a white stairway descended from this light. Our Great Grandmother walked down the stairs and looked at my sister. She told my sister that something was going to happen to our Grandfather but everything would be okay. She asked my sister to watch over our Mother and again reassured her that everything would be all right. She then smiled and turned around to head back up the glowing stairs. With each step she took, a step would disappear behind her. When Tracy woke up, she told me about her dream. Three days later, our Grandfather had a massive heart attack which required surgery. Our Mother took the news very hard but thanks to our Great Grandmother's message we watched over our Mother and helped her through the coming months. Our Grandfather recovered from his surgery and lived for many years after that.

Water helps us understand our Emotional and Dream Energy.

West/Water

The Element of Water helps all Seekers go between worlds using their dreams. Water shows us the messages we need to better understand our path.

Water is most sensitive to gossip and when Ego Cords are present in a Seekers energy.

Common Blocks:
Gossip
Worries
Emotional ups and downs

Ocean Cords

Key Characteristics of Ocean Cords:

These Cords are normally presented to me as a string of bright, dark blue ocean-coloured Cords followed by an image of the open ocean. The Energy is usually emphasized if the reader or Seeker hears the ocean in his/her ear during the reading. Ocean Cords symbolize a very intense dream energy state for these Seekers. Their dreams are usually quite profound. It can also indicate that the Seekers are having a difficult time sleeping.

This can also suggest that the Seeker is from the ocean or has a very strong connection to the ocean. If there is a flash of pink or a pink Cord, it can mean that this Seeker's soulmate is from the ocean or has a very strong connection to the ocean.

This is excellent energy for any Seeker who wants to investigate past lives through meditations or past life regressions.

The Guardians do say that if the water energy appears on the right side of the Seeker, it represents a male energy. When on the left side of the Seeker, it represents a female energy. This applies to all Energy Cords.

Food to eat: Sea food and sea vegetables

Energies to avoid: Malls and gossip

Psychic Exercise:

If you live near the ocean, try and do this exercise as often as you can. If you do not live near the ocean, create a sacred space that invites the ocean into your home. An altar of sea shells, a bowl of salt water, etc.

Taking three very deep breaths, focus your energy until you feel very grounded and clear. When you have your centre, invite the Guardians of the Ocean and your Guardians to your energy.

Visualize a ball of ocean embracing you. You may feel the room become a bit cool.
Then focus your energy, imagine it breaking like a spider's web, connecting every part of you to the ocean.

Listen.

Give Thanks. (Give out Tobacco or Milk)

River Cords

Key Characteristics of River Cords:

These Cords usually take on the appearance of a silver blue rope. It's a little bit thicker than the other Cords, but smaller then the Mountain Cord. During the reading the Seeker or reader may hear the rush of water similar to the sounds a river makes. River Cords represent movement for the Seeker and they also indicate that the Seeker is ready for a change. There is a lot of cleansing and the Seeker is letting go of the old.

River energy helps us let go of any energy we have outgrown.

It can also indicate that the Seeker is from the river or has a very strong connection to the river. If there is a flash of pink or a pink Cord, it can mean that this Seeker's Soulmate is from the river or has a very strong connection to the river.

Food to eat: River salmon or river trout

Energies to avoid: Violent movies or scary movies

Psychic Exercise:

Sitting in a quiet room, take a very deep breath until you feel that you cannot possibly inhale any more air. Hold your breath while focusing on the past. Exhale. Taking a second deep breath, hold it and focus on the present. On your third breath, focus on the future.

Focus your energy until you are grounded. Then focus it to connect with the closest river near your home. Invite the river to send its energy to you so that you may clear your aura.

Be sure to give thanks when you visit the river. Pick up any litter near the river and give thanks with milk, tobacco or bird seed.

Lake Cords

Key Characteristics of Lake Cords:

These Cords are usually a flash of a water body, almost like a clear bowl or bright blue water. The Guardians usually show this when they want the Seeker to be still and listen to information that has already been given to them. This is typically a time of reflection for the Seeker.

This can also indicate that the Seeker is from the lake or has a very strong connection to the lake. If there is a flash of pink or a pink Cord, it can mean that this Seeker's Soulmate is from the lake or has a very strong connection to the lake.

Food to eat: Cucumbers

Energies to avoid: Being online or on the computer for extended periods

Psychic Exercise:

If it is nice outside, this is a great exercise to do outdoors.

Focus your energy until you are grounded. Then focus your energy to connect with the closest lake near your home. Invite the Lake Guardians to send their energy for you to receive any messages. Many birds are very connected to lakes. Be sure to pay extra attention to surrounding birds while doing this exercise.

Be sure to give thanks when you visit the lake. Pick up any litter near the lake and give thanks with offerings of milk, tobacco or birdseed.

Rain Cords

Key Characteristics of Rain Cords:
You can normally see rain drops in the Seeker's aura. It is as if there is a little rain storm occurring in their Aura. It tells the reader that the Seeker is going through an intense time. The reader should look at other Cords surrounding the Rain Cords to help give the Seeker guidance that will help balance the rain.

Food to eat: Watermelon, honeydew melons, cantaloupes

Energies to avoid: New projects

Psychic Exercise:

When you are in the shower, focus on your energy until you feel very still and calm.
Ask the Guardians of the water for their help. Focus your energy on what is causing you any stress or worry. Visualize this, stressful energy as green (ie, green slime) Green will help heal this energy. Visualize this 'slime' coming out of your aura and being washed away with the 'rain' shower water.

Give thanks. **Offer water to the grass**

Energy Cords

North/Earth

On February 4th, 2006, our Father came home from his daily walk and told us that he had stumbled upon a new book store he thought we would like. My sisters Tracy and Kim and I bundled up and walked down the street to investigate this new store. The doors had just opened a half hour earlier and we were the first customers. The store, Sarah's Spiritual Treasures, is near my home in Lower Sackville, Nova Scotia. After meeting Sarah and her husband Tom, I asked if I could read out of their store and Sarah agreed. As our friendship blossomed, Sarah taught me wise grounding methods and a great deal about crystals. Until I met Sarah, I did not connect with Crystals or understand how to use them. Now I use crystals on a daily basis to help connect with Earth.

Earth helps us understand our physical Energy.

North/Earth

The Element of Earth helps keep Seekers grounded and focused on the tasks at hand. Earth helps us to heal and manifest the best possible outcome.

Common Blocks:

Expectations
Frustrations
Being impatient

Mountain Cords:

There usually represented by a thick grey stone rope followed by an image of a mountain in your mind's eye. Sometimes the Seeker may feel his/her room go cold and may feel the Guardians place a blanket or coat over them. Mountain Cords represent accomplishment. It suggests the Seeker has just overcome a major obstacle and should be rewarding herself for her hard work.

This can also suggest that the Seeker is from the mountains or has a very strong connection to the mountains. If there is a flash of pink or a pink Cord it can mean that this Seeker's soulmate is from the mountains or has a very strong connection to the mountains.

Key Characteristics of Mountain Cords:

Food to eat:

• Oatmeal

Energies to avoid: Negative words

Psychic Exercise:

Go outside, close your eyes, and ask the Divine to guide you to a stone that will help you. Open your eyes and focus until they rest upon a stone. If it is small enough, pick it up and give thanks. It if is larger, go over and place your hands on it.

Visualize white light surrounding you and connecting you to this stone.
Give thanks for the mountain's help.

Return the stone. Give thanks. A message may be given. Mountain energy is usually very quiet, so please be aware of everything being presented to you.

Tree Cords

Key Characteristics of Tree Cords:

These Cords are usually presented in several ways. It is important for the Seeker and the Reader to focus on what's being presented first.

If a tree root is presented first, then the Seeker is working on becoming more grounded. The Seeker may also be called to work on environmental issues. If the reader feels as though the root is trying to intertwine with the Seeker's Cords, this may mean that the Fairy realm is trying to reach out to them.

If the trunk of the tree is presented first, the Seeker is being asked to acknowledge his/her strength. The readers or Seekers may hear the Tree Guardians drumming in their ears. They may also smell pine needles.

If the branches of the tree are presented first without the body of the tree, this suggests the Seeker feels the need to gather more information. However the Seeker does not consciously know why he wants to gather this information. He feels as though there is missing information but they cannot pinpoint what information is missing. This is an excellent time for the Seeker to take a new class or seek out a teacher.

If a whole tree is presented first, then the reader should note what type of tree and ask the Seeker to keep an eye out for that particular tree and what it means to the Seeker. A whole tree represents an understanding, although it will happen through hard work. This means nothing was given to the Seeker. They had to work for it.

If a seed, acorn, or leaf is presented, the Seeker is in a new chapter of his/her life and should be very conscious of all words or actions. The Seeker should be reassured that it's okay to ask for help.

Food to eat: Swiss chard, rhubarb

Energies to avoid: Malls and crowds

Psychic Exercise:

Using a drum or a drumming CD

Focus your energy on the closest tree. Visualize an Energy Cord from your heart Chakra to the tree's heart. Ask for permission to connect with this tree. You should feel a gentle energy returned for yes or a firm energy sent back for no.

While you are drumming or listening to a drumming CD, feel the energy on each beat vibrate from your heart to the tree's heart.

Stay in this energy until you feel you have received the message you need.

Give thanks. You can place your hand on the tree and give thanks and/or pour milk on the tree's roots.

Earth Cords

Key Characteristics of Earth Cords:

These Cords are usually presented as a green orb or green haze surrounding the Seeker. The Divine is asking the Seeker to slow down and enjoy the moment. It may be wise for the Seeker to eat more fresh green vegetables and beans. (Guardians really enjoy green peas and beans.)

The Guardians may ask the Seeker to either save their money or to let go of worries about money.

Food to eat: Any root vegetables, beans and lentils.

Energies to avoid: N/A

Psychic Exercise:

Find a potted plant in your home and place it in front of you.

Visualize a green light surrounding you and the plant. Ask the plant's permission to connect with it. You should feel a gentle energy returned for yes, or a firm energy sent back for no.

Place both of your hands on the leaves and focus your energy on the plant. You may also gently rub the leaves. Plants enjoy this.

Ask the plant if there is anything they wish you to know.

Focus on all energy.

Give thanks. Egg shells to the potted plant are very much appreciated.

Snow Cords

Key Characteristics of Snow Cords:

These Cords can be represented as chains of snow flakes linked together surrounding the Seeker, or may appear as one huge snowflake. The Divine usually presents these when the Seeker has a strong connection to winter and snow. The Guardians sometimes advise the Seeker to look into skiing or skating for fun.

Food to eat: Snow cones and ice cream

Energies to avoid: N/A

Psychic Exercise:

Find a snow globe.

Holding the globe, in your hands visualize snow gently falling down around you.

Shake the snow globe, and hold it up and stare through it. Ask your Guardians and Guardians for any messages.

Give thanks.

Spirit

When I was 17 or 18 years old, I was given the chore to rake up the leaves in our backyard. I was having your typical teenage tantrum because I was given this task and was slacking off and mentally complaining quite loudly. Then a "Booming Energy" from the trees gently scolded me for my lack of respect. They stated that it was every Soul's Divine Duty to show respect to all Souls regardless of their physical form. He asked me if he had ever disrespected me and my heart replied 'no'. Then he asked me to give respect while tending to the Earth for she is a Soul too.

Spirit helps us understand our Divine Energy.

Moonlight Cords:

These Cords are presented as a thin hair the colour of moonlight. Sometimes you'll see a flash of light and then a strong image of a full moon in your mind's eye. This can symbolize that the Seeker before you is or was a priest or priestess in this life or in one of their past lives.

This is an intense spiritual energy. The Seeker is usually guided to study the Moon Signs (i.e. if the moon is in Aries or how moon phases affect people). It's also wise for the Seeker to spend some time on their own because moon energy can make people very sensitive to other energies. This Seeker should also avoid busy malls and gossip.

Key Characteristics of Moonlight Cords:

- Intensely drawn to the Moon
- Meditations

Food to eat:

- Milk

- White Rice
- Soy Milk
- Bread

Energies to avoid:

- Crowds
- Keep Sunday for you and your family
- Avoid shopping and restaurants

Psychic Exercise:

On a clear night, focus outside or at a picture window facing the Moon. Note what phase and sign the moon is in.

Visualize a Moonlight Cord connecting you to the moon. Humbly ask the moon for a dream about Who you are and what you are meant to do in this life.

Give thanks with milk.

Place a moonstone under your pillow and pay close attention to all your dreams for the next week.

If you do not dream, then you have the message that you need for now.

Star Cords:

These Cords are fairly rare. These Cords are not actual Cords but instead are very tiny stars surrounding the Seeker. The Seeker is working with an energy where they feel they are an outsider looking in. For the Seeker, it's a time for observation and listening.

Dreams may be very vivid.

Key Characteristics of Star Cords:

Food to eat: Mushrooms

Energies to avoid: Alcohol and drugs (and avoid people who do drugs)

Psychic Exercise:

On a cold and clear winter night, have a cup of tea and sit in a picture window watching the stars.

Pay attention to your thoughts.

Give thanks.

Rainbow Cords:

This Cord represents a rainbow flashing before the Seeker. It suggest to me that the Seeker is in a "peacemaker" position. If the rainbow follows the Seeker into the room, it may mean that the Seeker is still working to forge a truce with a close friend or family member. It also means that this Seeker is willing to fight for peace for the highest good.

It also means that this seeker has the ability to form a team where everyone works together peacefully and to their full potential.

Key Characteristics of Rainbow Cords:

Food to eat:

- Any fruit
- Apple juice

Energies to avoid: Never assume the truth. Ask.

Psychic Exercise:

Focus a 'Rainbow' Cord from your Third Eye to surround you and your loved ones.
Focus on your Soul's truth, that the one you wish to share with them.

Next time you are speaking to your Guardians, listen closely to their words for confirmation that they received your message.

Give thanks.

Crystal Cords

These Cords are usually presented by the Guardians as a rope made of crystal. The crystal presented to me is the crystal they are asking the Seeker to work with. Sometimes the reader and/or the Seeker may feel as if the Guardians are placing a crystal in their hands during the reading.

On occasion they may present homework with that cord to either strengthen it or suggest a place of focus. For example, if someone needs to look into journalism they will put that energy in the cord by showing a newspaper or writing pad.

Seekers are always guided to trust their own intuition when working with crystals, unless the Guardian has a specific message.

Food to eat: Whatever you are currently craving.

Energies to avoid: Shopping

Psychic Exercise:

Holding a crystal of your choice, focus your energy on clearing the crystal. You should feel a calm peaceful energy when the crystal is cleared.

Envision a white light connecting your Third Eye to the crystal. Ask the crystal if you may connect your energy to its energy. You should feel a gentle energy returned for yes or a firm energy sent back for no.

Work with the crystal's energy to connect with the Guardians around you.

Give thanks. Put your crystal in the sunlight or moonlight.

Ice Cords

Key Characteristics of Ice Cords:

These Cords are usually a sheet of ice representing the Seeker's sense of "being stuck." This is usually presented to the Seeker from the Divine, asking the Seeker to have more patience. It is wise to advise the Seeker to have faith.

Food to eat: Ice, ice cream, snow cones or yogurt.

Energies to avoid: Excessive heat.

Psychic Exercise:

Place an ice cube in a large clear bowl. Fill the bowl with cold water.

Watch the ice as it melts. The shape it takes is the message.

Return the water to the earth and give thanks.

Spirit Cords

Key Characteristics of Spirit Cords:

Spirit Cords are very rare. They are usually a combination of Fire Cords, Water Cords, Crystal Cords and Sky Cords.

They are highlighted with light purple and gold rays that glows through the Cord. This is what I call a very high Cord. It suggests that the Seeker is in a very sacred place. The Seeker has a great deal of healing, and/or spiritual work to do for others. The Divine usually advises the Reader to strongly encourage such Seekers to trust their intuition.

This Seeker has many decisions before them, but has the wisdom to walk this path.

Food to eat: Anything organic

Energies to avoid: N/A

Psychic Exercise:

Build an altar or sacred space. Be sure to have the four elements represented. Most commonly this is a Candle for fire, a bowl of water for water, crystal for earth and incense for air.

Closing your eyes, focus on your aura and see how it is presented to you.

Push your energy away from your body so you are embracing the whole room. Be sure to pay attention to how the energy reacts to the room.

Humbly Ask the Divine for a message and give thanks.

Ego Cords Quiz

Question 1:

How are you handling your anger?

You are:

(A) Blaming others
(B) Blaming yourself
(C) Jealous of other Soul's success
(D) Feeling the need to control the situation
(E) Feeling the need to gather more information or that you are missing something.
(F) Feeling you made the wrong decision
(G) Not Sure

If you answer:

(A) You are in a Gossip Cord
(B) You are in a Fear Cord
(C) You are in a Judgement Cord
(D) You are in a Manipulation Cord
(E) You are in an Assumption Cord
(F) You are in a Regret Cord
(G) Please go to question 2

Question 2:

Why are you Frustrated?

(A) You should have your wish by now
(B) You feel you have no psychic abilities

If you answer:

(A) You are in an Expectation Cord
(B) You are in a Worries Cord

Ego Cords

When I was in elementary school, I remember not understanding the other children. When I looked at them I would be in awe of their Soul's Light. So many of them had such beautiful energies that I could not wait to become friends.

However, whenever I tried becoming friends with them I became painfully shy. Whenever I spoke awkwardly, a brown muddy haze would surround them and the child would mock me or say very hurtful words.

I became very confused, because the energy that these children were sharing with me was not who they truly were.

I decided that if I didn't speak, the muddy haze would not appear as strongly and I wouldn't be so hurt.

Even though my social life in elementary, junior high and high school was very painful, I am profoundly grateful. Because of these experiences, I have learned three very important things:

1. When a Soul forgets him/herself it can become something it is not

2. No Soul needs another Ego's approval

3. When someone's words or actions hurt you, you have a right to say no and walk away from that Ego without hurting or offending that Soul. **(Ego is not the Soul)**

Second Story:

In 2006 I lost my voice completely. I began having gaps in my spoken words.
In February it progressively got worse. By the summer, I had lost my voice completely. This lasted for two weeks. I called this period 'two weeks of silence.'

During the two weeks of silence I meditated and asked my Guardians why had I lost my voice.

At first I heard nothing. There was no obvious message given to me. For three days I rested and watched TV. I was in my heart at peace with my lost of voice but my family was very worried. I knew that there was a reason for this and when the time was right I would understand.

On the fourth day a Guardian came and told me in a dream that I needed the Energy of 'stillness and silence'. He said I had to quiet my Soul in order to truly hear the Guardians' messages. He then told me because I speak between worlds I needed to learn to really listen to what is **not** being said.

When I woke up the next day I felt renewed and began writing out what I wished to teach Seekers.

Even though this was a time that created a few frustrations, it became a beautiful crossroads for me. **One does not need to speak to be heard.**

~~~~~~

What is Ego?

My understanding of Ego, is that it exists to teach us what we are not. Ego is an energy that lacks faith in yourself and/ or the Divine.

Here are a few basic tips on how to balance all Ego Cords:

Remember Laughter breaks all Ego Cords

If someone is complaining, gossiping or judging others they may have too much ego.

To help, they need to focus on the positive.

Examples:

Sue is complaining about a co-worker. You can instead give that co-worker a positive compliment.

If you go for a psychic/intuitive reading and the reading leaves you upset or frightened, ask the Guardians to clarify the source of your fear. It is often an over reaction or an egotistic misinterpretation. The Guardians never use fear to pass on a message.

Example:

Take your fear and visualize it to give it a physical form (i.e. mud or dirt). Gently stomp your feet to shake out the Ego Energy. Keep doing this until you feel a peace.

Also remind yourself that you have a right to a beautiful and positive life. Tell your Ego that you will not settle for nothing less.

*** Another Note: These Ego Cords may not be necessarily coming from you. You may be feeling these Cords coming from someone else. To determine whether they are yours or another Soul's Ego, ask your heart. If you listen you will know. ***

Importance Of BREAKING the Ego Cords:

A path for the intuitive is not unanimous. It is created within a Soul's Heart.

Ego is like a master teacher showing the Soul everything they are not. Breaking Free from Ego takes patience forgiveness and integrity. You must use your own powers to see your truth.

We must understand that Ego need not be hated or feared. But realize that Ego is a teacher.

First Ego Exercise.

1. Using your visual powers, imagine how your Ego looks to you

2. Give him/her/it a voice and personality

3. Taking very deep breaths, visualize white or gold light surrounding you

4. Invite your Ego into your circle

5. Explain to your Ego what it is about yourself that you are unhappy with (VERY important to be accountable for YOUR actions. This exercise is not to BLAME your Ego, but to learn from it)

6. Invite your Guardians into your circle.

7. Humbly ask everyone for guidance

8. Give thanks

We are not our Ego.

Egos are:

*   Very Loud
*   Rude
*   Hurtful
*   Jealous
*   Unaccountable for their actions

How do we know when our Egos are speaking and NOT our Soul's light?

The energy you receive will make you scared. It will make you worry.

Ego Cord: Fear

Key Characteristic of Fear Cord

Fear is the root of all Ego. A Fear Cord is an energy that is telling you that you can't do something because of an apprehension of a possible outcome that may or may not exist.

Fear tells us that we 'don't deserve,' 'can't' and 'will never' have happiness, etc.

Food to eat: Any fresh Green Vegetables.

Energies to avoid: Anything that feeds your fear ie watching scary movies, any one who is pessimistic.

Psychic exercise

Fear denies who we are. When you are feeling the energy of fear you are giving away your power. To help heal your own fears, embrace them. Treat your fears as a lonely child who wishes to be understood. This is one psychic exercise that you must create from your own strength. Know that you do have the power to break all fears. Never doubt that.

1. Identify your Fear. What is the root of this Fear?

2. Give your Fear a symbol--i.e. a sword, a voice, etc.

3. Express your Fears to this symbol. Have a conversation with it.

4. Call in your Guardians and ask them to help you heal this Fear.

5. Take a deep breath, focus on your heart until you feel your own inner strength to let go of this Fear.

6. Tell your symbol that you are Fearless and give thanks to your Guardians.

Ego Cord: Assumptions

Assumptions can be very dangerous. They are not necessarily the truth.

When we can't let go of the past it is usually because of our assumption. Assumption blocks our Throat Chakra (this Chakra is about communication and the truth). This is why our throats may feel tight when we think about a situation that we believe was handled unfairly. Assumptions are either a conscience or unconscious denial of seeking the truth.

Key characteristics of Assumption Cords

*   A feeling that something is 'missing'
*   Can't let go of the stress or worries created from a situation.
*   You may feel anger/frustration/hurt but don't know why

Food to eat: Red Apples or Apple Sauce

Energies to avoid: All Gossip and any second hand information.

Psychic exercise

Become a detective and seek the truth. This can mean asking a few uncomfortable questions. You may even feel that you are not sure if you want to know the truth but to take back your power, you must find the truth in every situation. Remember the Divine wants you to be happy and to understand your own path. Whatever message presented to you (whether you perceive it as positive or negative) has a purpose.

1. Identify the validity of the information that you are being given by others. I.E. is this first hand facts or hearsay?

2. Know that you have the courage and honor to ask for the absolute truth.

3. If the truth is not the best outcome you were hoping for, know that when you seek the truth, a seed of truth will be planted in your aura. This will be your light to the next part of your path.

Ego Cord: Gossip

Key Characteristics of Gossip Cord

When we speak unkindly about someone we manifest a haze in our Energy Cords that can hinder our own psychic sight.

To walk a path of True Soul's Light, we must be true to ourselves and the other paths of Soul.

There is a difference between 'venting' an Ego Cord and being disrespectful to someone.

Venting your Ego Cord is when you are accountable for your own Ego and speak or write about what frustrated you in a specific situation. For example, "I am upset by this person's actions."

Being disrespectful is when we play the "victim card" meaning that we feel sorry for ourselves or another. We do not see our own power or the power of the person in the situation.

Food to eat: Blueberries

Energies to avoid: Gossip, rumors or anyone who thrives on telling tales.

Psychic exercises:

• Someone is gossiping to you:

This takes a bit of practice because you don't want to create more **Ego Haze** by making the other person(s) feel that you think you are better than them.

Scenario #1:

A group of co-workers are complaining about a 'lazy' co-worker.

First read the energy to see if there is any truth to these accusations. If in your heart you feel this is an unfair assessment, and that you feel that your co-worker does not deserve this, speak up and say so. When speaking the truth in an Ego Haze, keep your words very gentle and kind. Any awkward energy from the co-worker who is speaking is their own Ego Cord. Ask your Guardians to help clear the energy around you.

Share a compliment about the co-worker everyone is complaining about to put their focus on the Soul's light.

• You have 'gossip' to share:

Ask yourself two things before sharing:

1. Is it your place to say anything?

2. Will this news hurt someone?

If you say no to question one, respect the other person and honor your Soul's light and say NOTHING.

If you answer Yes to question 2. Say NOTHING.

You catch yourself 'gossiping' before you can stop yourself.

Egos can be very loud. This is the hardest Gossip Ego Cord to 'break' because you may feel guilty after you have spoken.

The second you realize that your words are hurtful to someone else or that it is not your place to share this news you should stop talking. Apologize to the person(s) you are speaking with and be accountable.

For Example: "I am so sorry, I should not have said this. If so-and-so heard, it would hurt their feelings."

Example 2: "I am sorry it is not my place to share this news."

Egos can feed each other too. The other person's Gossip Cord may be a bit strong and encourage you to keep talking. Use your strength to keep with your Soul's light, and change the subject.

Ego Cord: Worries

Key Characteristics of Worry Cords

When we worry, we experience a lack of faith. As you already know, what you think is what you will become.

You focus only on negative outcomes. Worries will block our sight & acts as a distraction.

Food to eat: Oranges or Lemons

Energies to avoid: Anything that feeds our worries

Psychic exercise

This does take practice. Please don't expect yourself to be worry free for life. This is a life long lesson, and it takes dedication to help understand and master it.

When you catch yourself worrying, take a deep breath and think 'I have faith in my right to be joyful' (You can word this any way that fits the worry. It is better to create your 'worry cancelling technique' to reflect your power.)

Another exercise is to keep telling yourself 'I have faith' over and over until you feel the worry energy 'break'

Give thanks.

Ego Cord: Expectations

Key Characteristics of Expectation Cords

Expectations will limit your experience with the Divine. There are many Seekers out there who feel that they are doing something wrong or feel that they don't have any psychic abilities.

In March 2008 my sisters and I started looking to buy our house. We turned to Tarot to help us get an idea when we would find the ideal home.

We pulled the 7 of Cups. At first we were like 'Fantastic! We will have our house in 7 days, 7 Weeks or 7 Months'

7 days went by no house.
7 weeks went by no house.
7 Months went by no house.

So we went to Tarot again and asked. We pulled the 7 of Pentacles.

Again we were like 'Fantastic! We will have out house in 7 days, 7 Weeks or 7 Months'

7 days went by no house.
7 weeks went by no house.
7 Months went by no house.

We were getting caught up in our disappointment and we decided to take a break from house hunting. We change our focus to business.

In January 2010, we felt is was time again to get serious about finding our house. So we consulted the Tarot. The 7 of Cups came up again.

We were like "Okay... We get it..."

After two offers rejections we bought our happy house in May. However we did not move until July, 2010. The 7th Month... Tarot was right. However because we were limiting the Tarot with our expectations, we were missing the message.

Food to eat: Beans

Energies to avoid: Having an expectation during any readings or psychic exercises.

Psychic exercise

It is easy to miss expectations. The best way to notice whether you are in an 'expectation' is to ask yourself:

"Are you really letting go of all control and allowing the Divine decide the outcome?"

When doing a reading or meditation, trust whatever is presented to you and put it in the back of your mind.

When the time comes for that message to present or manifest itself you will have a higher understanding of its meaning.

Ego Cord: Frustrations

Key Characteristics of Frustration Cords

When we become frustrated we lose sight of what is before us.
Frustrations are created when we feel that we are 'behind' in some way.

For example after a day of readings, I got off work. My bus stop is literally right in front of the Little Mysteries Book Store. As I stepped out, my bus was already at the stop. As I tried to hurry to get on, it pulled away. I was really frustrated because had I not stopped for idle chit chat, I would not have missed my bus.

My frustration grew into a bit of anger. I was 'stewing' by the time the next bus came 10 minutes later.

After taking a few very deep calming breaths, I reminded myself that the Universe probably had a reason for this and reminded myself to keep my eyes open for the message.

After getting off the bus, a good friend of mine happened to be driving along the street and spotted me. She pulled over to chat. I heard all about her beautiful trip to South America. I was really inspired by her journey. It encouraged me to do a bit of research.

Later that day, upon reflection I realized that this is what the Universe needed me to see. Had I gotten the earlier bus, I would have missed this experience.

Food to eat: Chocolate (yes I said Chocolate)!

Energies to avoid: The situation or person (people) creating the frustration.

Psychic exercise

In a moment of frustration, realize that you are frustrated, but gently remind yourself that there is a reason for it. Have faith that it will present itself when the time is right.

If someone else is Frustrated:

Read the energy very carefully before saying anything.

If this person is becoming angry it may not be the best time to say "There is a reason for this." It could make them more angry because they may feel that you are not taking them seriously.

Let them vent for a moment and find something humorous in the situation. Once the person is laughing gently remind them that there is a reason for this.

Ego Cord: Regrets

Key Characteristics of Regret Cords:

Regrets are the Divine's way of letting us know we are going against our Soul's Light (Our intuition)

When a past regret keeps 'haunting' a Seeker, it is very important for that Seeker to look into which actions were responsible for creating the regret.

Food to eat: Bread or Crackers

Energies to avoid:

Psychic exercise: The 'Seeds' of Regret Exercise

1. Write a list of regrets

2. Ask yourself *why* you chose Ego over Soul's light. Be very honest with yourself.

3. What were you afraid of? Did you feel you were being respected during the situation?

4. Find the 'balance'. Did the situation hurt anyone else besides yourself? Was their dishonesty or an assumption given instead of your truth? Tell the truth to anyone who was not told the whole story. This can be hard because you are admitting that you were wrong. By owning your actions and being accountable for the energy you will FREE yourself from your EGO

5. Forgive yourself. There is a reason for this and every experience

6. Reward your hard work. This could be with flowers, chocolate, etc.

7. Smile and be happy

Cords we all have

Mercury Cord

These Cords are represented by silver light. The Guardians present these Cords when the Seeker has a gift with words. The Guardians usually present either books, a computer and/or magazines to show the Seeker what medium he/she should focus on or use.

The Seekers tend to be an avid writers and usually write their wisdom in a journal. If the Cord comes from the back of the Seeker, it means that the Seeker has remembered an important past life and has written it either as a child or maybe she/he has an idea for a book. The Guardians usually encourage the Seeker to get writing.

Exercises for Mercury Cord

Get a subscription to the newspaper. Either local or national or both. Read the newspaper EVERY day. Not online because we can become distracted by our emails or social media but the actual paper.

The Mercury Cord works best when the paper is placed before you and your physical eye can be directed by your Mercury Cord to the words that your Guardians feel you need to read. I understand that some Seekers feel that reading the news can feel a bit negative given the upsetting events and actions from around the world. But know this: You have the power and ability to send healing love to everyone involved.

Knowing what is going on in the world can help you read the energy better. If you go to work and you feel the energy is off but can not understand why, you could be picking up the 'Echo Cord'. By knowing that you are picking up an Echo Cord you can gently send back the energy in love and light and send healing thoughts and energy to everyone.

Abundance Cord

This Energy Cord helps the Seeker understand that he/she has the right to all abundance. (Health/Love/Wealth) There is no set description of this cord. Just the feeling of worthiness that the Seeker experiences.

To help strengthen these cords I offer three exercises

Health

Focus your Soul's Light and visualize a beautiful healthy body. Feel and know your beauty.

Call in your Ego and gently tell it that you are healthy and that any blocks that have been created will lovingly be let go.

See what is presented to you. Be sure to pay extra attention to any symbols or food.

Give Thanks

Love

Stand before a mirror. In your reflection look yourself in the eye and feel your beauty.

Speak out loud that you are lovely and deserve nothing but love.

Yes, it is that simple.

Wealth

If you feel that the financial abundance surrounding you never stays this may be a good exercise for you.

Whenever you spend money, make sure that this money has already been earned and is not something that you feel entitled too.

For example:

If you use your credit card when you could have saved for a big purchase, or you have food at home yet chose to use your credit card to buy fast food, you have created an imbalance or 'pull' within your abundance cord.

It is important to strengthen your Wealth Energy by earning what you buy. For nonessential items, have the money saved.

Please note that this does not include long term debts such as mortgages, car loans etc.

Beauty Cord

This Energy Cord is how the Seeker sees his/her beauty. I have noticed during many readings that this cord does not match the Seekers Soul's Light. Some souls do not see or believe in their own beauty and strength.

This is a major psychic block. When you do not believe in your beauty, you forget who you are.

To help see your beauty, begin giving yourself treatments that affirm your right to let your beauty shine.

At home Beauty Treatment:

*** Remember to test any treatments on a small patch of skin to make sure that you won't have any adverse reactions***

You Need:

Plain Yogurt
Small bowl
Spoon

The yogurt represents Moonlight. The Moon shines in the dark, helping us to see what is truly there, not to fear it.

Take a spoonful of yogurt and place it in your hand. As you hold it focus your Soul's Light and know that you are beautiful.

Use your fingers to gently spread the yogurt over your clean face and neck.

Once the yogurt is spread over your face, using two fingers gently make small circles all over your face. As you do this, know you are beautiful and deserved this beauty treatment as a reminder of your beauty inside and out.

Wisdom Cord

This Energy Cord is how the Seeker sees his/her wisdom. Many Seekers underestimate their wisdom or settle, choosing not to expand what they already know.

To help strengthen this cord, find a subject that interest you.

For example

Canadian History.

Every day read and/or study something new about this subject.

Another great psychic exercise is to learn a new language. Every day or week, learn a new word in your chosen language.

Write it out 10 times and try to speak a sentence in your chosen new language.

Physical/Strength Cord

The Physical Cord is how the Seeker sees their own strength.

This psychic exercise is also a physical exercise.

**** Prior to any physical exercise, be sure to consult a Physician***

Here is the Physical Ritual I do everyday:

What you will need:

Free Weights
1 lbs to 10 lbs, depending on your level of fitness. You don't
<u>need</u> the weights

Jumping rope

Create your own Physical/Strength Cord Ritual:

Example:

100 Crunches
100 jumping jacks
100 kicks each leg
10 push ups

Bonus Psychic Exercise

To help connect your Energy Cords to the Element with
which you wish to connect, turn your bed so that the top of
your head is facing the direction you wish to work with.

Example:

If you wish to increase more psychic energy in your life, turn
your bed facing South. Before you sleep, humbly ask your
Guardians to connect your energy to that direction to help
increase the flow of that Element.

East = Air (communications)

South = Fire (Spiritual)

West = Water (Love)

North = Earth (Abundance)

Chakra	Location	Function
Crown	Top of Head	Spiritual Knowledge, Thinking
Third Eye	Between your two eyes	Intuition
Throat	Your Throat	Speaking your Truth, Communication
Heart	Around your Breast Bone	Matters of the Heart, Self Love & Love for Others
Solar Plexus	By your Belly Button	Your Power, Confidence
Sacral	Approximately three inches from your belly button	Creativity, Sexual & Material Desires
Root	Base of your Pelvis	Grounding, Basic Needs, Survival & Security

How to Raise Golden Circle

Taking a deep cleansing breath, imagine your Soul's Cord breaking free from your heart. Visualize this Cord dispersing from your body, embracing every inch of you.

Take another breath from your Soul's Cords, humbly calling in The Divine.

(This is my Personal Prayer to The Divine. Please feel free to use it or make your own.)

Great Guardians Of The:

East and Air
South and Fire
West and Water
North and Earth

Above, Below, Within.

Sunlight, Moonlight and Starlight

Plant, Mineral, Animal Kingdom

Angels, Fairies, Power Animals

Guardians, Guides, Ancestors,

Goddess Brigit, Goddess Maat, Goddess Isis, Goddess Kali, Goddess Venus, Mars, Merlin, Jesus, Buddha, Mother Mary Jupiter, Saturn, Mercury Goddess Kuan Yin

God and Goddess

I humbly Pray to serve you, The Divine, The Seeker, My Family and Soulmate.

Basic Psychic Exercises

Cutting old Energy exercise

This is one of the more effective ways to release old energy that you may have outgrown.

It is recommend that this exercise be done once a day.

What you will need:

1. A timer
2. Something or a room in your home to clean

The psychic exercise:

1. Use your intuition to find a room where you feel the energy needs cleansing.

2. For example: If you feel your personal life needs a change, focus on your bedroom. Start by cleaning out any drawers, closets, shelves, etc.

3. Set your timer to 15 minutes.

4. Clean the space that you chose for exactly 15 minutes, this way it does not become a chore.

Basic Candle Psychic Exercise for Fire

What you will need:

-   A dark quiet room
-   Any candle of your choice
-   Candle holder
-   Lighter or matches.
-   A table

The psychic exercise:

1. Find a comfy chair/couch/floor.

2. Take the Candle in your hands and humbly ask the Guardians or whomever you are connected to help clear your Third Eye to help you see better. For the highest good.

3. Next set the candle in the candle holder.

4. Set the candle holder and candle on the table then light the candle.

5. Turn off any lights so that the only source of light is from the candle flame.

6. Sit yourself in front of the candle light in a comfortable position.

7. Gaze into the flame and soften your eyes so that you may see 'Cords' of light breaking from the flame.

Advanced Candle Psychic Exercise

What you will need:

- A Dark quiet room
- Any candle of your choice
- Candle holder
- Lighter or matches
- A table

The psychic exercise:

1. Find a comfy chair/couch/floor.

2. Take the candle in your hands and humbly ask the Guardians or whom ever you are connected to help clear your third eye to help you see better. For the highest good.

3. Next set the candle in the candle holder.

4. Set the candle holder and candle on the table then light the candle.

5. Turn off any lights so that the only source of light is from the candle flame.

6. Sit yourself in front of the candle light in a comfortable position.

7.   Gaze into the flame and soften your eyes so that you may see 'Cords' of light breaking from the flame.

8.   Ask your Guardians for a message

9.   Close your eyes.

10. Focus on the 'darkness' behind your eye lids.

11. Receive the message.

Glossary

Cord The Energy Path that comes from the Soul or Divine that connects us to everything.

The Different Cords

Echo Cord The residual of energy cord that has since past.

Ego appears to be a Fear based Energy but is a Master teacher to show all Soul's what they not.

Ego Haze Energy that can block the third eye

Equal Energy What we say and/or give to another soul is equal to what is said and/or received back.

Golden Circle A concentration of the Seeker's energy creating a sacred space to communicate with the Guardians and understand the Energy Cords.

Reading Interpreting the Energy Cords and messages from the Guardians.

Seeker anyone Seeking a Higher Understanding of themselves and this world.

Soul's light The True energy of every Soul. Include the animal kingdom and mineral kingdom

Bibliography

Amy Zerner and Monte Farber, The Instant Tarot Reader. St. Martin's Press, 1997

Amy Zerner, The Enchanted Tarot. 2000

Barbara G. Walker, The Woman's Encyclopedia of Myths and Secrets. Harper Collins, 1983

Doreen Virtue, Ph.D., Goddess and Angels. Hay House, 2005

Doreen Virtue, Ph.D., Healing with the Angels. Hay House, 1999

Doreen Virtue, Ph.D., Realms of the Earth Angels. Hay House, 2007

Doreen Virtue, Ph.D., The Lightworker's Way. Hay House, 1997

John Holland, 101 ways to Jump-start you Intuition. Hay House, 2005

Nigel Suckling, Faeries of the Celtic Lands. Facts, Figures & Fun, 2007

Patricia Mercier, The Chakra Bible: The Definitive Guide to Chakra Energy, Sterling 2007

Robert Kirk, The Secret Commonwealth of Elves, Fauns and Fairies. Dover Publications, 2008

Great websites to check out

Ann Costello, author of Her Candle Burns at Both Ends
www.anncostello.com

Dr. Fronie LeRoy is a great Doctor of Oriental Medicine.
www.BaiduTCM.com

Gina Gammon Artwork, Artist of beautiful water colour
paintings.
www.ginagammon.com

Jenny Marie, Lower Sackville, Nova Scotia, Intutive Psychic,
working to empower her Seekers. 902-252-0621

Little Mysteries, Halifax, Nova Scotia Canada
www.littlemysteries.com

Phyllis Laforest, is a beautiful Psychic Reader and Reiki
Master in Nova Scotia
www.onewhitedove.net

Sarah's Spiritual Treasures, Lower Sackville, Nova Scotia
www.sarahsspiritualtreasures.com

Sogo Body Therapy, takes an all natural approach to
personal beauty and well being.
www.sogo.ca

The Ryan Sisters, Please check out their beautiful music!
www.ryansisters.com

Tracy Hinschen, is a gifted intuitive artist, Nova Scotia,
Canada
www.tracyhinschen.com

How to find Kelliena

Twitter: www.twitter.com/Kelliena

Facebook: Kelliena Psychic Readings

Website: www.kelliena.com